# So you think you know Welsh Sport?

## *Welsh Sports Quiz*

# MATTHEW JONES

Cover illustration: Sion Jones

ISBN: 9781847711267

Printed on acid-free and partly recycled paper
and published and bound in Wales by
Y Lolfa Cyf., Talybont, Ceredigion SY24 5AP
*e-mail* ylolfa@ylolfa.com
*website* www.ylolfa.com
*tel* (01970) 832 304
*fax* 832 782

# So you think you know
## Welsh Sport?

# Introduction

Although small in size and population, Wales has over the years punched above her weight when it comes to the landscape of world sport. In fact, sporting success can be easily argued as the country's greatest tool in promoting herself on foreign soil.

John Charles, Ian Rush and Ryan Giggs are amongst many Welshmen who would easily have enhanced any country's football team. How would the Great Britain rugby league side have fared without the likes of Jim Sullivan, Gus Risman or Billy Boston?

People harbour back to the rugby union successes of the 1970s, but the Grand Slam scalps of 2005 and 2008 re-enforce the fact that Wales will always be sat at the sport's top table. Could you imagine the history of the game without the outside half factory that produced the likes of Cliff Morgan, Barry John and Phil Bennet?

Lynn Davies' leap in the 1964 Olympic Games is the most iconic moment in the Welsh athletic story; however, the likes of Colin Jackson and Tanni Grey-Thompson have done more than their fair share in claiming international acclaim. In the ring, Joe Calzaghe has recently followed the likes of Jimmy Wilde and Howard Winstone into the boxing vaults of fame.

From Ray Reardon to Ian Woosnam, Tony Lewis to Carl Llewellyn, success has been widespread. Here's your opportunity to see if you remember who did what or maybe when?

**Matthew Jones**

# Round 1

1. **Football. Who played his 750<sup>th</sup> and final game for Everton in a 2-0 loss to Tottenham Hotspur on the 29<sup>th</sup> of November 1997?**

   a) Neville Southall

   b) Barry Horne

   c) Kevin Ratcliffe

2. **Rugby Union. Who captained Wales to their 2008 Grand Slam victory?**

   a) Ryan Jones

   b) Huw Bennett

   c) Ian Gough

3. **Athletics. Colin Jackson set a world record for the 110m hurdles in the World Championship in Stuttgart in 1993. This record stood until 2004. What was his time?**

   a) 14.91

   b) 13.91

   c) 12.91

4. **Snooker. In 1988, who won the UK Championship?**

   a) Darren Morgan

   b) Doug Mountjoy

   c) Terry Griffiths

5. **Boxing. Who beat Joe Bowker for the British featherweight title on the 28th of May 1906?**
    a) Jim Driscoll
    b) Freddie Welsh
    c) Francis Rossi

6. **Cricket. Which Glamorgan player made his England test debut against Pakistan in the summer of 1996?**
    a) Steve James
    b) Robert Croft
    c) Dean Cosker

7. **Rugby League. During Great Britain's 1974 tour down under, who became the first Welshman to be selected for test Rugby as a back and a forward?**
    a) Jim Mills
    b) David Willicombe
    c) Colin Dixon

8. **Swimming. Who won a silver medal in the 200m butterfly at the 1968 Olympic Games, beating legend Mark Spitz in the process?**

9. **Football. Peter Nicholas left Crystal Palace in a £500,000 move in March 1981. Which fellow London club signed him?**

10. **Rugby Union. Name the 3 Pontypridd players to appear for Wales at Full back in the 1997 calendar year?**

# Round 2

1.  **Rugby Union. Graham Henry became Welsh coach in 1998. Which country was he from?**

    a) New Zealand

    b) Canada

    c) Ireland

2.  **Football. Who guided Real Madrid to the Spanish league title with a record number of points and goals in the 1989/90 season?**

    a) Alan Curtis

    b) Joey Jones

    c) John Toshack

3.  **Golf. Which Welshman won the 1991 US Masters?**

    a) Stephen Dodd

    b) Phillip Price

    c) Ian Woosnam

4.  **Showjumping. David Broome won his first World Championship in 1970. What was the name of his horse?**

    a) Mozart

    b) Beethoven

    c) Handel

5. **Cricket. Who made a Glamorgan record of 34,056 runs in 610 first class appearances between 1957 and 1983?**

    a) Jim Pressdee

    b) Tony Lewis

    c) Alan Jones

6. **Boxing. Who beat Willie Ritchie to become world lightweight champion in 1914?**

    a) Ivor Thomas

    b) Freddie Welsh

    c) David Owens

7. **Snooker. Ray Reardon lost his only World Championship final in 1982. Who was the victorious player on this occasion?**

    a) Alex Higgins

    b) Cliff Thorburn

    c) Steve Davis

8. **Rugby League. During the 1930s, which 17 times capped Great Britain centre three-quarter, won three Championships and a Challenge Cup with Salford?**

9. **Football. GQ magazine named which Welsh international as their 'man of the year' in 1998?**

10. **Rugby Union. Who was Wales' first captain in the 21st century?**

# Round 3

1. **Rugby Union. Onllwyn Brace, Brynmor Williams and Robert Jones were Welsh internationals known for playing in which position?**

   a) Scrum Half
   b) Second Row
   c) Prop

2. **Football. Who became Wales' youngest ever player at the age of 18 years and 71 days against Northern Ireland in 1950?**

   a) John Charles
   b) Frank Scrine
   c) Keith Jones

3. **Athletics. In 2000, who became the third Briton to win a European 200m indoor title?**

   a) Doug Turner
   b) Christian Malcolm
   c) Kevin Williams

4. **Boxing. Joe Calzaghe recorded a points victory over Roy Jones Junior in November 2008. At which famous venue was the fight held?**

   a) Boardwalk Hall, Atlantic City
   b) Madison Square Garden, New York
   c) Caesars Palace, Las Vegas

5. **Cricket. In 1937, who set a Glamorgan record of 176 wickets during a single season?**

    a) Jack Mercer

    b) Austin Matthews

    c) Johnnie Clay

6. **Rugby League. Gorseinon born Lewis Jones made the 'move North' in 1952 for a then record fee of £6,000. Which club did he join?**

    a) Wigan

    b) Leeds

    c) Hunslet

7. **Formula One. Tom Pryce was tragically killed in the South Africa Grand Prix of 1977. Which team was he driving for at the time?**

    a) Ferrari

    b) Shadow

    c) Lotus

8. **Athletics. In the 1986 Commonwealth Games, which female became a double gold medallist in the 800m and 1500m?**

9. **Football. Who became the League of Wales' record transfer in a £25,000 move from Caernarfon Town to Barry Town in 1997?**

10. **Rugby Union. Name the two Celtic Warriors players to have captained Wales before the region was disbanded.**

# Round 4

1. **Rugby League. Who won the accolade of 'Man of steel' as the best player in Super League for 1999?**

   a) Lee Briers

   b) Keiron Cunningham

   c) Iestyn Harris

2. **Rugby Union. Which club provided all three members of the back row – Emyr Lewis, Scott Quinnell and Mark Perego for Wales' 1994 Five Nations campaign?**

   a) Pontypridd

   b) Neath

   c) Llanelli

3. **Football. Mark Hughes scored both goals in Manchester United's 2-1 victory in the 1991 European Cup Winner's Cup final. Who were the Spanish opposition?**

   a) Barcelona

   b) Athletico Madrid

   c) Real Zaragoza

4. **Golf. David Thomas, Dai Rees and Brian Huggett share which Golfing connection?**

   a) Open Championship winner

   b) Open Championship runner up

   c) US Masters winner

5. **Cricket. Glamorgan's 1948 County Championship wining side was captained by which former rugby union international?**

   a) Wilf Wooller
   b) George Lavis
   c) Phil Clift

6. **Boxing. Who won lightweight gold at the 2002 Commonwealth Games in Manchester?**

   a) Lee Jones
   b) Darren Edwards
   c) Jamie Arthur

7. **Rugby Union. Who directly preceded Gareth Edwards in the Welsh number 9 shirt?**

   a) Allan Lewis
   b) Billy Hullin
   c) Clive Rowlands

8. **Snooker. Name the two Welshmen in the final of the 1999 UK Championship.**

9. **Football. Who made his Premiership debut in Arsenal's final game of the 1999/2000 season against Newcastle United?**

10. **Athletics. The 1998 Commonwealth Games saw Wales claim a bronze medal in the shot put. Which Abersychan born athlete won the medal?**

# Round 5

1. **Football. What was the relationship between internationals Ivor and Len Allchurch?**
    a) Brothers
    b) Father and son
    c) Cousins

2. **Rugby Union. In 2003, who became the first player, unattached to a club or region side to captain Wales?**
    a) Mark Taylor
    b) Scott Quinnell
    c) Colin Charvis

3. **Cricket. Garry Sobers famously scored 6 sixes in an over for Nottinghamshire at St Helen's in 1968. Who was the unlucky Glamorgan bowler at the receiving end of this feat?**
    a) Tony Cordle
    b) Malcolm Nash
    c) Don Shepherd

4. **Athletics. For which country did Lynn Davies became Technical director for Athletics, in 1973?**
    a) Australia
    b) Jamaica
    c) Canada

5. **Darts. Leighton Rees became British Darts Organisation (BDO) world champion in 1978. Which Englishman did he defeat in the final?**

   a) Bobby George
   b) Eric Bristow
   c) John Lowe

6. **Rugby Union. In 1907, Jim Webb became the first international from which club side?**

   a) Abertillery
   b) Blaenavon
   c) Swansea

7. **Football. Which future England international goalkeeper won the LDV vans trophy with Wrexham, in a 2-0 victory over Southend United, in 2005?**

   a) Scott Carson
   b) Chris Kirkland
   c) Ben Foster

8. **Powerboating. Who won his 4th Formula One Powerboating World Championship in 1998?**

9. **Horse Racing. Who in 1992 won the Grand National on Party Politics?**

10. **Rugby Union. Which Neath player became the first person to be sent off in a World Cup match, as Wales lost 49-6 to New Zealand in 1987?**

# Round 6

1.  **Football. In 1991, who became the most expensive transfer in English football with his £2.9 million move from Derby County to Liverpool?**

    a) Colin Pascoe

    b) Dean Saunders

    c) Iwan Roberts

2.  **Rugby Union. How old was Barry John when he announced his international retirement in 1972?**

    a) 22

    b) 25

    c) 27

3.  **Athletics. Who were the two Welshmen who won silver at the 2006 European Championship in the British 4x400m relay team?**

    a) Matt Elias and Gareth Warburton

    b) Tim Benjamin and Rhys Williams

    c) Iwan Thomas and Jamie Baulch

4.  **Snooker. Who beat Darren Morgan in the final of the 1992 Welsh Open, the first time the event was a ranking tournament?**

    a) Stephen Hendry

    b) John Parrott

    c) Steve Davis

5. **Cricket. Glamorgan won the Norwich Union limited overs Division One title in 2002. Who was the county captain for that famous season?**

   a) Robert Croft
   b) Steve James
   c) David Hemp

6. **Rugby League. The Celtic Crusaders played their first ever Super League match against the Leeds Rhinos in February 2009. Who was their captain for this watershed occasion?**

   a) Josh Hannay
   b) Tony Duggan
   c) Jace Van Dijk

7. **Boxing. Freddie Welsh was born in Pontypridd in 1886. What was his real name?**

   a) Frederick Gwyn Jones
   b) David Frederick Davies
   c) Frederick Hall Thomas

8. **Football. Which player's international career did Terry Yorath finish, after he failed to turn up for a World cup qualifier against West Germany in 1989?**

9. **Rugby Union. Which Ebbw Vale centre captained his country on three occasions during the 1973 season?**

10. **Cycling. Who won Commonwealth bronze in the women's 25km point race at the Victoria games of 1994?**

# Round 7

1. **Boxing. In 2007, which Welshman was voted BBC Sports Personality of the Year?**
   a) Joe Calzaghe
   b) Gary Lockett
   c) Gavin Rees

2. **Football. At the age of 32, Chris Coleman became the youngest ever Premiership manager in 2003. Which club made this appointment?**
   a) Fulham
   b) Arsenal
   c) Chelsea

3. **Rugby Union. Who was Neath's only representative on the 1997 British and Irish Lions tour of South Africa?**
   a) Steve Williams
   b) Darren Morris
   c) Barry Williams

4. **Snooker. Who did Matthew Stevens defeat 10-8 to be crowned UK champion in 2003?**
   a) John Higgins
   b) Jimmy White
   c) Stephen Hendry

5. **Football. Who left Bolton Wanderers in October 1966 to join Newcastle United for an £80,000 club record fee?**

    a) Wyn Davies

    b) David Hollins

    c) Brian Godfrey

6. **Cricket. In which year did Glamorgan join the County Championship?**

    a) 1901

    b) 1911

    c) 1921

7. **Shooting. Who won gold at the men's 50m rifle prone, in the 2006 Commonwealth Games?**

    a) Ian Harris

    b) David Phelps

    c) Gruffudd Morgan

8. **Athletics. Who won a silver medal in the men's 1998 European Championships 200m final?**

9. **Rugby League. Who was the top points scorer in Britain for 13 seasons between 1922 and 1938?**

10. **Rugby Union. What was unusual about brothers Martyn and Charles Jordan's international careers?**

# Round 8

1. **Football. Who signed John Hartson in a £2.5 million deal for Arsenal in January 1995?**

     a) Bruce Rioch

     b) Stewart Houston

     c) George Graham

2. **Rugby Union. Who scored Wales' only try in their 23-15 victory over England in February 2009?**

     a) Mark Jones

     b) Leigh Halfpenny

     c) Matthew Rees

3. **Snooker. Which player was nicknamed Dracula?**

     a) Terry Griffiths

     b) Ray Reardon

     c) Cliff Wilson

4. **Horse Racing. Carmarthen horse owner and trainer Sirrell Griffiths won which event with 100-1 outsider Norton's Coin in 1990?**

     a) Grand National

     b) Cheltenham Gold Cup

     c) Welsh National

5.  **Darts. In which year did Richie Burnett become BDO World Champion?**

    a) 1991
    b) 1993
    c) 1995

6.  **Cycling. Nicole Cooke became the first Briton to win which women's event in August 2003?**

    a) World Cup
    b) Tour de France
    c) European Cup

7.  **Football. Who became the last Welsh side to play in the European Cup Winners Cup during the 1998/99 season, losing 3-0 over two legs to FC Haka of Finland in the first round?**

    a) Newtown
    b) Bangor City
    c) Caernarfon Town

8.  **Rugby Union. Viv Jenkins became the first Welsh full back to score an international try in 1934. Keith Jarrett was the second in 1967. Who was the third in 1970?**

9.  **Cricket. Who succeeded Wilf Wooller as Glamorgan captain in 1961?**

10. **Boxing. Which Ely boxer defeated Wilson Palacio to take the World Boxing Organisation (WBO) super featherweight belt in 1997?**

# Round 9

1. **Rugby Union. Pandy Park is home to which club side?**

   a) Swansea

   b) Newport

   c) Cross Keys

2. **Football. Ian Rush became the most expensive British footballer when he moved from Liverpool to Italy for £3.2 million in 1986. Which Italian club signed him?**

   a) AC Milan

   b) Roma

   c) Juventus

3. **Swimming. Which medal did David Davies win in the 10km swim at the 2008 Olympic Games?**

   a) Gold

   b) Silver

   c) Bronze

4. **Athletics. The 1980 Moscow Games saw the first Welsh woman win an Olympic Athletics medal, a bronze in the 4x400m relay. Who was she?**

   a) Sian Morgan

   b) Michelle Probert

   c) Carmen Smart

5. **Rugby Union. Jeff Young was Wales' ever present Hooker in their 1971 Grand Slam winning side. Which club side did he play for at the time?**

   a) Harrogate

   b) Gloucester

   c) Coventry

6. **Cricket. In July 1936, which bowler set a Glamorgan record of 10 wickets for 51 runs, against Worcestershire?**

   a) Jack Mercer

   b) Johnnie Clay

   c) Trevor Arnott

7. **Football. John Aldridge began his professional career with Newport County. Which Welsh Cup winning amateur side did the exiles sign him from?**

   a) West Kirby

   b) South Liverpool

   c) East Birkenhead

8. **Boxing. On the 23rd of January 1968, who defeated Mitsunori Seki in 9 rounds to become World Featherweight Champion?**

9. **Tennis. Which competition did Gerald Battrick win in 1964 that J.P.R. Williams also won two years later?**

10. **Rugby Union. Name the Swansea brothers who between them appeared at full back in 51 of Wales' first 102 internationals.**

# Round 10

1.  **Football. Craig Bellamy left West Ham in January 2009 to re-join former manager Mark Hughes. Which club paid £14 million for his services?**

    a) Real Madrid

    b) Manchester City

    c) Inter Milan

2.  **Rugby Union. Which former international centre, was Welsh national coach from 1974 to 1980?**

    a) Haydn Davies

    b) Cyril Davies

    c) John Dawes

3.  **Boxing. Joe Calzaghe defeated Peter Manfredo Jr in 2007. How had the American become so well known in his home country?**

    a) He was then President George W Bush's nephew

    b) He won reality television programme 'The Contender'

    c) He won Olympic gold at the Sydney games of 2000

4.  **Athletics. Tanni Grey-Thompson's first Paralympic medal was a bronze at the 1988 Seoul games. Which event was this medal achieved in?**

    a) 200m

    b) 400m

    c) 800m

5. **Rugby League. In November 1968, which Halifax player made a try scoring debut for both Wales and Great Britain in that same month?**

      a) Colin Dixon

      b) Ronnie James

      c) Wynford Phillips

6. **Snooker. Doug Mountjoy won the first of two UK Championships in 1978. Who did he defeat 15-9 in the final?**

      a) Dennis Taylor

      b) John Virgo

      c) Alex Higgins

7. **Football. Robbie James tragically died at the age of 40 from a heart attack while playing for which club side?**

      a) Barry Town

      b) Llanelli

      c) Merthyr Tydfil

8. **Rugby Union. Who scored the last ever points at Stradey Park in a victory over Bristol in October 2008?**

9. **Cricket. Which former Australian test Cricketer was named Glamorgan first team coach in 2000?**

10. **Bowls. Who won gold at the 1972 World Championship in Worthing?**

# Round 11

1. **Rugby League. St Helens stalwart Keiron Cunningham plays at which position?**

   a) Wing

   b) Hooker

   c) Full back

2. **Rugby Union. Who directly preceded Phil Bennet as Welsh captain?**

   a) John Dawes

   b) Mervyn Davies

   c) Gareth Edwards

3. **Football. Who became Cardiff City's youngest ever player at 16 years and 124 days, when he came on as a replacement against Hull City in April 2007?**

   a) Aaron Ramsey

   b) Joe Ledley

   c) Darcy Blake

4. **Cycling. Geraint Thomas' gold at the 2008 Olympic Games was won in which event?**

   a) Individual pursuit

   b) Team pursuit

   c) Points Race

5. **Athletics. Colin Jackson won silver in the 1988 Seoul Olympic Games. Who beat him to the gold?**

   a) Roger Kingdom

   b) Tonie Campbell

   c) Tony Jarrett

6. **Darts. Who were the World Darts Federation (WDF), World Cup, world pairs champions in 1997?**

   a) Eric Burden and Richie Herbert

   b) Sean Palfrey and Martin Phillips

   c) Marshall James and Ritchie Davies

7. **Football. Trevor Ford became Britain's most expensive forward in 1950 when he left Aston Villa for £30,000. Who signed him?**

   a) Newcastle United

   b) Preston North End

   c) Sunderland

8. **Snooker. Who defeated Joe Johnson in 1978 to become world amateur champion?**

9. **Basketball. Which South Wales female basketball side were the British league champions in 2001, 2004, 2005 and 2006?**

10. **Cricket. Name the Queensland bowler who became Glamorgan's overseas player for 2002.**

# Round 12

1.  **Football. Which former Manchester United and England international became manager of Bangor City in 2001?**
    - a) Bryan Robson
    - b) Danny Wallace
    - c) Peter Davenport

2.  **Rugby Union. The Memorial Ground is home to which club side?**
    - a) Glamorgan Wanderers
    - b) Cardiff
    - c) Pontypridd

3.  **Cricket. Which former Glamorgan batsman became Technical Director of the England and Wales Cricket Board in 1997?**
    - a) Alan Jones
    - b) Hugh Morris
    - c) John Hopkins

4.  **Football. 'Wild man of Borneo' was a nickname given by Bob Paisley to which player?**
    - a) John Toshack
    - b) Ian Rush
    - c) Joey Jones

5.  **Golf. Why did Ian Woosnam lose 2 strokes which potentially cost him the 2001 Open at Lytham?**
    - a) He hit a spectator accidentally with a golf club

b) His caddie Miles Byrne packed too many clubs in his bag

c) He mistakenly hit Greg Norman's ball instead of his own on the fairway

**6. Boxing. At which Cardiff venue was Freddie Welsh's much anticipated fight with Jim Driscoll held on the 20th of December 1910? This was a fight where the latter was infamously disqualified for head butting.**

a) Ninian Park

b) The American roller rink

c) Cardiff Castle

**7. Cricket. In 2000, who beat Glamorgan in the Benson and Hedges cup final?**

a) Sussex

b) Gloucestershire

c) Yorkshire

**8. Rugby Union. Prior to Cardiff's 8-3 victory over New Zealand in 1953, who was quoted as saying 'if we fail, we fail, but we have got to be different'?**

**9. Show Jumping. Name the Welshman who made his first Olympic appearance in 1960 and his final appearance 32 years later in 1992.**

**10. Various. What's the link between the 1965 Welsh Pole Vaulting Championship, and Wales' 1999 rugby union victory over England?**

# Round 13

1.  **Football. In 2008, Ryan Giggs' 759th appearance for Manchester United meant he'd played for the club a greater number of times than any other. Whose record did he break?**

    a) George Best
    b) Paul Ince
    c) Bobby Charlton

2.  **Rugby Union. Which former Outside Half was named Chief Executive of Cardiff RFC in 1994?**

    a) Gareth Davies
    b) Geraint John
    c) Barry John

3.  **Rugby League. In 1981 a side was established in South Wales that attracted high profile players including Steve Fenwick and Tommy David. What were they called?**

    a) Cardiff Blue Dragons
    b) Aberavon Red Roosters
    c) Potypridd Green Devils

4.  **Athletics. Neil Winter became a gold medallist in the 1994 Commonwealth Games. In which event did he win this honour?**

    a) High Jump
    b) Pole Vault
    c) Discus

5. **Snooker. Mark Williams became World Champion for the second time in 2003. Who did he defeat 18-16 in the final?**
   - a) John Higgins
   - b) Ronnie O'Sullivan
   - c) Ken Doherty

6. **Football. Gordon Davies set a club record of 178 goals in 448 games during the 1970s and 1980s. For which English club?**
   - a) Queens Park Rangers
   - b) Fulham
   - c) Chelsea

7. **Boxing. Mal Pope's musical 'The Contender' was based on the life of which boxer?**
   - a) Jim Driscoll
   - b) Idris Pugh
   - c) Tommy Farr

8. **Rugby Union. Name the two Welshmen that started every test match for the British and Irish Lions' unsuccessful tour of Australia in 2001.**

9. **Cricket. Which Pakistan bowler was Glamorgan's overseas signing in their County Championship winning season of 1997?**

10. **Swimming. Which female became a double bronze winning medallist in the 100m backstroke and 100m freestyle relay at the 1932 Los Angeles Olympic Games?**

# Round 14

1. **Boxing. Frank Bruno lost to Lennox Lewis in the first all British, heavyweight world title fight in 1993. Which stadium hosted the event?**

   a) Rodney Parade, Newport

   b) National Stadium, Cardiff Arms Park, Cardiff

   c) Richmond Park, Carmarthen

2. **Football. Which of the following did not play under Graeme Souness at Benfica in the late 1990s?**

   a) Dean Saunders

   b) Mark Pembridge

   c) Marcus Browning

3. **Rugby Union. In Wales' 19-17 defeat by Australia in 1978, at which position did J.P.R. Williams start the game?**

   a) Outside Half

   b) Hooker

   c) Flanker

4. **Rowing. At the 1958 Empire and Commonwealth Games held in Cardiff, where was the rowing event held?**

   a) Llyn y Fan

   b) Llyn Padarn

   c) Usk reservoir

5. **Football. Jack Kelsey began his career with which Swansea league side?**

   a) Gendros
   b) Pontardawe
   c) Winch Wen

6. **Rugby League. Which Welshman captained the Northern Union's first ever test side to a 22-22 draw against Australia in 1908?**

   a) Johnny Thomas
   b) George Ruddick
   c) Bert Jenkins

7. **Rugby Union. Second Row Derwyn Jones left Cardiff in 1999 for a final season in France. Which side did he join?**

   a) Beziers
   b) Dax
   c) Pau

8. **Athletics. Who was named World Junior Athlete of the year in 1998?**

9. **Cricket. Which former Zimbabwean captain became Glamorgan coach in 1997?**

10. **Speedway. Who was crowned world speedway champion in 1950 and 1953?**

# Round 15

1. **Rugby League. Saturday 21st February 2009 saw the Celtic Crusaders play their first ever home match in Super League, a 20-28 loss to Hull FC. At which ground was the match played?**

   a) The Brewery Field, Bridgend

   b) The Racecourse, Wrexham

   c) Sardis Road, Pontypridd

2. **Football. Matthew Le Tissier scored 48 goals from 49 penalty kick attempts. Which goalkeeper saved his one and only failure?**

   a) Mark Crossley

   b) Neville Southall

   c) Tony Norman

3. **Boxing. British, Commonwealth and European bantamweight champion Johnny Owen, was known by which nickname?**

   a) Owen the punch

   b) The matchstick man

   c) The Merthyr terrier

4. **Rugby Union. In 1988, who captained Wales to a first Triple Crown in nine years?**

   a) Paul Thorburn

   b) Robert Norster

   c) Bleddyn Bowen

5. **Horse Racing. At which event did Sam Thomas ride Denman to victory in 2008?**
   a) Grand National
   b) Cheltenham Gold Cup
   c) Welsh National

6. **Rugby Union. John Bassett became the 50th person to lead the national side in March 1930. Which club side did he play for?**
   a) Neath
   b) Penarth
   c) Aberavon

7. **Squash. Who won Commonwealth bronze at the 1998 Kuala Lumpur games, in the men's singles?**
   a) Alex Gough
   b) Gavin Jones
   c) David Evans

8. **Athletics. Berwyn Price set a Welsh record for most Great Britain appearances with a total of 50 by 1982. Who previously held the record with 43?**

9. **Football. What did Joey Jones win in 1983, which Eddie Niedzwiecki won in 1986 and Mark Hughes won in 1997?**

10. **Rugby Union. Who was the only Pontypool player to captain Wales during the 1970s?**

# Round 16

1. **Football. Who infamously missed a penalty in Wales' 2-1 defeat to Romania on Wednesday 17th of November 1993?**
   - a) Paul Bodin
   - b) Ian Rush
   - c) Barry Horne

2. **Rugby Union. Lynn Howells became head coach of which club side in 1999?**
   - a) Bridgend
   - b) Cardiff
   - c) Llanelli

3. **Athletics. 'Seize the day' is the autobiography of which Welsh athlete?**
   - a) John Harris
   - b) Chris Hallam
   - c) Tanni Grey-Thompson

4. **Snooker. Who became the first Welshman in 18 years to become Benson and Hedges Masters champion in 1998?**
   - a) Darren Morgan
   - b) Mark Williams
   - c) Matthew Stevens

5. **Cricket. In which year did Glamorgan play their first match at Sophia Gardens?**

    a) 1967

    b) 1972

    c) 1977

6. **Rugby Union. Wales recorded a 50-6 victory over Samoa in November 2000. Which substitute became the first Welshman to earn a yellow card on his debut during that game?**

    a) Deiniol Jones

    b) Nathan Budgett

    c) James Griffiths

7. **Rugby League. Tommy Harris scored 69 tries in 507 first class games of Rugby League. Which club side did he play for throughout his professional career?**

    a) Widnes

    b) Hull

    c) Oldham

8. **Badminton. Which female defeated India's Aparna Popat to win singles gold at the 1998 Commonwealth Games?**

9. **Football. Who became the first Welshman to manage Everton in January 1994?**

10. **Boxing. Joe Erskine became British heavyweight champion in 1956, by defeating another Welsh fighter at Maindy Stadium. Who did he defeat?**

# Round 17

1. **Rugby League. Which Wigan legend scored a phenomenal 478 tries in 488 appearances for the club between 1953 and 1968?**

   a) Gwynne Davies

   b) Don Hayward

   c) Billy Boston

2. **Football. In September 1997, who became the first person to make 200 Premiership appearances?**

   a) David Phillips

   b) Neville Southall

   c) Mark Bowen

3. **Boxing. Joe Calzaghe joined the stable of a well known promoter in 1997, and stayed with him until 2008. Who was this promoter?**

   a) Barry Hearn

   b) Frank Maloney

   c) Frank Warren

4. **Rugby Union. Who captained his country in his 46th and final international appearance, a 19-17 defeat by Australia in June 1978?**

   a) Steve Fenwick

   b) Graham Price

   c) Gerald Davies

5. **Cricket. What piece of history did Robert Croft claim on the 12th of September 2007?**

  a) Highest wicket taking Glamorgan bowler with 2219 wickets

  b) First Welshman to achieve 10,000 first class runs and 1,000 wickets

  c) First player to claim 6 wickets in a 20-20 match

6. **Football. Park Avenue is the home of which club side?**

  a) Cwmbran Town

  b) Bangor City

  c) Aberystwyth Town

7. **Weightlifting. Which event did Michaela Breeze win gold in, at the 2002 Commonwealth Games?**

  a) Snatch

  b) Clean and Jerk

  c) Combined

8. **Rugby Union. Hal Luscombe, Rhys Thomas and Ian Evans were all born in which African country?**

9. **Cycling. Which female sprinter won gold at the 1990 Commonwealth Games in Auckland?**

10. **Football. Leighton Phillips won the league cup in 1975 and 1977. Which Midlands club did he play for at the time?**

# Round 18

1. **Football. Which club side did Tony Pulis lead into the Premiership in 2008?**
   - a) West Bromwich Albion
   - b) Stoke City
   - c) Liverpool

2. **Athletics. Which of the following did not win a silver medal at the 1996 Olympic Games in the 4x400m relay?**
   - a) Paul Gray
   - b) Jamie Baulch
   - c) Iwan Thomas

3. **Rugby Union. The Scarlets lost 16-18 to Munster in their first game at Parc y Scarlets. Who scored the side's first ever points at the stadium during this game?**
   - a) Stephen Jones
   - b) Ceiron Thomas
   - c) Rhys Priestland

4. **Snooker. Which of the following is not from Tredegar?**
   - a) Ray Reardon
   - b) Cliff Wilson
   - c) Dominic Dale

5. **Football. Alan Curtis is the nephew of which fellow former Welsh international?**

    a) Roy Paul

    b) George Lowrie

    c) Mal Griffiths

6. **Rugby League. Jonathan Davies spent the summer of 1991 playing in Australia. Which club did he join?**

    a) Sydney Roosters

    b) Brisbane Broncos

    c) Canterbury Bulldogs

7. **Rugby Union. Wales defeated South Africa for the first time, 29-19 in 1999. Who were the two try scorers for the home team?**

    a) Mark Taylor and Gareth Thomas

    b) Peter Rogers and Dafydd James

    c) Robert Howley and Chris Wyatt

8. **Darts. Who became BDO world champion at the Lakeside in 2008?**

9. **Football. Which manager took Ian Rush to Newcastle United in 1997?**

10. **Cricket. In 1993, who partnered West Indies legend Viv Richards to a Glamorgan 4$^{th}$ wicket record of 425 not out against Middlesex?**

# Round 19

1.  **Football. How many games did Wales win during Vinnie Jones' 9 cap career in the mid 1990s?**

    a) 0

    b) 1

    c) 9

2.  **Golf. Who captained Europe to victory in the 2006 Ryder Cup?**

    a) Stephen Dodd

    b) Ian Woosnam

    c) Phillip Price

3.  **Rugby Union. Who was Wales' ever present Fly Half in their 1976 Grand Slam campaign?**

    a) John Bevan

    b) Phil Bennett

    c) Gareth Davies

4.  **Boxing. In 1937, which Welsh heavyweight took the legendary Joe Louis the distance at New York's Yankee Stadium in front of a crowd of 32,000, before losing on points?**

    a) Tommy Farr

    b) Dai Davies

    c) Jack Jones

5. **Various. Barry Memorial Hall was used as a venue for the 1958 Empire and Commonwealth Games. Which event did it host?**

    a) Weightlifting
    b) Wrestling
    c) Fencing

6. **Rugby League. St Helens defeated Leeds 16-13 in the 1972 Challenge Cup final at Wembley. Who captained the St Helens team and won the Lance Todd trophy?**

    a) John Mantle
    b) Kel Coslett
    c) Roy Mathias

7. **Rugby Union. Who scored the only try in New Zealand's 12-3 victory over Wales in 1974?**

    a) Sid Going
    b) Ian Kirkpatrick
    c) Bryan Williams

8. **Football. Who is the only player in the 20th century to have won the FA Cup on 4 occasions?**

9. **Athletics. Who won a silver medal at the 2002 Commonwealth Games in the 400m hurdles?**

10. **Rugby Union. In 1997, who became the first and only Pontypridd player to captain Wales in a 28-25 victory over Canada?**

# Round 20

1. **Rugby Union. What is the name of Pontypool's home ground?**
   a) Pontypool Parade
   b) Pontypool Road
   c) Pontypool Park

2. **Football. Which Brazilian scored his first ever World Cup goal in his country's 1-0 win over Wales in the 1958 quarter final match?**
   a) Didi
   b) Pelé
   c) Zagalo

3. **Boxing. Swansea's Enzo Maccarinelli lost his second ever professional fight in March 2008. In doing so he lost his WBO cruiserweight title. Who was his victor?**
   a) Mark Hobson
   b) Bobby Gunn
   c) David Haye

4. **Snooker. Who in 1996 became the first Welshman to win the Welsh Open as a ranking competition?**
   a) Mark Williams
   b) Darren Morgan
   c) Dominic Dale

5. **Horse Racing. Talgarth born Geoff Lewis won the 1971 Derby. What was the name of the horse he rode?**
   a) Mill Reef
   b) Lupe
   c) Right Track

6. **Football. Ryan Giggs made his international debut as a substitute in a 4-1 loss to Germany in 1991. Who did he replace for the last six minutes of the match?**
   a) Ian Rush
   b) Eric Young
   c) David Phillips

7. **Cricket. Which touring side did Glamorgan beat at St Helen's in August 1951?**
   a) Australia
   b) New Zealand
   c) South Africa

8. **Athletics. Who won gold in the 30km walk at the 1982 Commonwealth Games in Brisbane?**

9. **Football. Which London side paid a club record fee of £7.5 million for John Hartson in January 1999?**

10. **Rugby Union. Who scored the British and Irish Lions only try in their decisive 19-18 victory over Australia in the final 1989 test?**

# Round 21

1.  **Rugby Union. Gethin Jenkins, Mike Griffiths and Graham Price are all internationals who have played at which position?**

    a) Prop

    b) Second Row

    c) Outside Half

2.  **Cycling. Which medal did Nicole Cooke achieve in the 2002 Commonwealth Games' road race?**

    a) Gold

    b) Silver

    c) Bronze

3.  **Football. Andy Dibble saved a Nigel Winterburn penalty to help his side to a 3-2 victory over Arsenal in the 1988 League Cup final. Who did he play for?**

    a) Nottingham Forest

    b) Manchester City

    c) Luton Town

4.  **Boxing. Which former European welterweight champion managed a stable of boxers that included Howard Winstone, Ken Buchanan and Eddie Avoth?**

    a) Gwyn Williams

    b) Eddie Thomas

    c) Cliff Curvis

5. **Cricket. Which Glamorgan player was made a member of the 'Gorsedd' at the 1997 National Eisteddfod?**

   a) Hugh Morris

   b) Darren Thomas

   c) Robert Croft

6. **Rugby Union. Which Ebbw Vale player captained Wales' development tour of Canada in 2000?**

   a) Mark Jones

   b) Nathan Budgett

   c) Richard Smith

7. **Rugby League. What was remarkable about Great Britain's second test match against New Zealand in 1958?**

   a) First time the entire pack consisted of Welshmen

   b) First ever Great Britain side not to include a Welshman

   c) Seven Welshmen took to the field breaking the previous record of five

8. **Football. Who was named Italian Football player of the year in 1958?**

9. **Athletics. Who won 6 consecutive British AAA Championship 110m hurdles titles from 1973 to 1978?**

10. **Rugby Union. Which club provided a then record ten players for the Welsh side that drew 3-3 with England in 1948?**

# Round 22

1.  **Football. Aaron Ramsey made a £5 million move from Cardiff City to London in the summer of 2008. Which club did he join?**
    a) Chelsea
    b) Arsenal
    c) Tottenham Hotspur

2.  **Athletics. Which former athlete came second to Darren Gough in the 2005 series of BBC's 'Strictly Come Dancing'?**
    a) Iwan Thomas
    b) Colin Jackson
    c) Kirsty Wade

3.  **Rugby Union. Who broke his own record for fastest international Welsh try, when he crossed the whitewash after 33 seconds in a 26-25 defeat by Ireland in 1997?**
    a) Ieuan Evans
    b) Simon Hill
    c) Wayne Proctor

4.  **Golf. What did Ian Woosnam and David Llewellyn do in 1987, which Bradley Dredge and Stephen Dodd also did in 2005?**
    a) Gain selection for the Ryder Cup
    b) Win a Masters tournament
    c) Win the World Cup

5. **Snooker. Who did Steve Davis beat in the final of the 1981 World Championship at the crucible?**

    a) Doug Mountjoy

    b) Terry Griffiths

    c) Ray Reardon

6. **Rugby Union. Wales lost 6-3 in their first international following the First World War. Who was the opposition?**

    a) New South Wales

    b) Royal Air Force

    c) New Zealand Army

7. **Rowing. In the 1932 Olympic Games, Hugh Edwards became the second man to do what in rowing?**

    a) Win four gold medals

    b) Win two gold medals on the same day, in the coxless pair and coxless four

    c) Win gold in three consecutive games, in the coxless eight

8. **Football. Whose first game in charge of Wales was a 4-1 victory over England at The Racecourse in 1980?**

9. **Rugby Union. Name the three Neath players that formed the Welsh front row in Wales' 13-9 loss to Scotland in 1990.**

10. **Boxing. In 1995, which loudmouth Englishman defeated WBO featherweight champion Steve Robinson in Cardiff?**

# Round 23

1.  **Rugby Union. Cliff Morgan, Barry John and Jonathan Davies are all legendary players at which position?**

    a) Wing

    b) Flanker

    c) Outside Half

2.  **Horse Racing. Former Grand National winning jockey Hywel Davies is from which West Wales town?**

    a) Milford Haven

    b) Cardigan

    c) Fishguard

3.  **Rugby League. Luke Dyer created history on Friday the 6th of February 2009. What did he do?**

    a) Scored the Celtic Crusaders first ever try in Super League

    b) Became the first ever Celtic Crusaders player to be sin binned in the Super League

    c) Became the first non Welshman to play for the Celtic Crusaders

4.  **Football. Who was the only Welshman to be included in the list of inaugural inductees to the English Football Hall of Fame in 2002?**

    a) John Charles

    b) Billy Meredith

    c) Ian Rush

5. **Rallying. Co-driver Phil Mills became the first Welshman to clinch which prize in 2003?**
   a) World Rally Championship
   b) British Rally Championship
   c) Wales Rally of Great Britain

6. **Boxing. Who won featherweight bronze at the 2006 Commonwealth Games?**
   a) Robert Turley
   b) Matthew Edmonds
   c) Darren Edwards

7. **Rugby Union. Trelyn Park is home to which East Wales side?**
   a) Senghenydd
   b) Fleur De Lys
   c) Monmouth

8. **Athletics. Which future rugby union international scrum half was Welsh schools champion at the high jump in 1969 and 1970?**

9. **Football. Who scored the winning goal in Wales' 2-1 win over Hungary in their World Cup quarter final play-off match in 1958?**

10. **Cricket. Despite losing in the 2000 Benson and Hedges cup final, which Glamorgan player was so exceptional that he was awarded the accolade of 'man of the match'?**

# Round 24

1. **Snooker. What was the prize money when Doug Mountjoy became UK champion in 1978?**
   a) £700
   b) £7,000
   c) £70,000

2. **Rugby Union. Who scored 41 points in 3 tests during the 1997 British and Irish Lions tour of South Africa?**
   a) Adrian Davies
   b) Arwel Thomas
   c) Neil Jenkins

3. **Rugby League. Wales recorded a 68-0 victory over Papua New Guinea at The Vetch Field in 1991. Who contributed 24 of those points?**
   a) Rowland Phillips
   b) Jonathan Davies
   c) David Young

4. **Football. In which city, was 13 times capped Pat Van Den Hauwe born?**
   a) Dendermonde, Belgium
   b) Geldorp, Netherlands
   c) Montpellier, France

5.  **Boxing. Which flyweight in 1914 defeated England's Bill Ladbury to become Wales' first ever boxing world champion?**

    a) Tommy Lewis
    b) Lewis Williams
    c) Percy Jones

6.  **Rugby Union. Which club side drew 3-3 with Australia on the 21$^{st}$ of December 1908?**

    a) Pontypridd
    b) Ebbw Vale
    c) Abertillery

7.  **Gymnastics. At which event did David Eaton win Commonwealth silver at the 2006 games in Melbourne?**

    a) Parallel bars
    b) Horizontal bars
    c) Pommel Horse

8.  **Football. Ryan Giggs became the 8$^{th}$ person to make 100 appearances in the Champions League on the 20$^{th}$ of February 2008. Who was the only British player to have achieved this sooner?**

9.  **Cricket. Which Glamorgan player made his England test debut against South Africa in 1998?**

10. **Rugby Union. During the 2008 Grand Slam campaign, who scored the Welsh tries against England at Twickenham?**

# Round 25

1. **Rugby Union. Mike Ruddock became head coach of which English side in the summer of 2007?**
    a) Worcester
    b) Bristol
    c) Bath

2. **Football. Which 45 times capped Republic of Ireland international was born in Builth Wells on the 21st of October 1959?**
    a) John Aldridge
    b) Kevin Sheedy
    c) Ray Houghton

3. **Athletics. Which track event at the 1994 Commonwealth Games in Victoria, Canada, saw Wales claim a gold and bronze medal?**
    a) Men's 400m
    b) Women's 800m
    c) Men's 110m hurdles

4. **Rugby League. Salford paid a world record fee of £15,000 to Halifax in 1968. Who did they purchase?**
    a) David Jones
    b) Johnny Freeman
    c) Colin Dixon

5. **Darts. Richie Burnett lost 6-3 in the 1996 BDO World Championship final. Which Englishman was victorious in this match?**

     a) Steve Beaton

     b) Mervyn King

     c) John Walton

6. **Football. Cardiff City reached the semi-final of the 1967/68 European Cup Winners' Cup. Which German side defeated the Bluebirds 4-3 on aggregate?**

     a) Bayern Munich

     b) Hamburg

     c) Borussia Dortmund

7. **Cricket. Who was Glamorgan's top wicket taker in their successful 1993 Sunday League campaign?**

     a) Steve Watkin

     b) Roland Lefebvre

     c) Steve Barwick

8. **Rallying. Which North Walian claimed the prize of British rally champion in 1996?**

9. **Rugby Union. Name the three players who formed an all Swansea back row in Wales' 51-0 defeat to France in 1998.**

10. **Boxing. Newport's Mo Nasir won bronze at the 2006 Commonwealth Games. Which weight category did he contest?**

# Round 26

1. **Rugby Union. Following the creation of regional rugby in Wales, which side did Gavin Henson join from Swansea in 2003?**

   a) Celtic Warriors

   b) Neath Swansea Ospreys

   c) Llanelli Scarlets

2. **Boxing. 'I'm not a flash bloke. I'm prudent and some might say tight' is a quote attributed to which former world champion?**

   a) Enzo Maccarinelli

   b) Joe Calzaghe

   c) Gavin Rees

3. **Football. Cwmbran Town are known by which nickname?**

   a) The Eagles

   b) The Crows

   c) Blue Finches

4. **Snooker. The first Benson and Hedges Masters final in 1975 was a tight affair, decided on a re spotted black. Who defeated Ray Reardon in this match?**

   a) John Spencer

   b) Perrie Mans

   c) Cliff Thorburn

5. **Rugby League. For 4 consecutive seasons between 1922 and 1926, Johnny Ring finished as top try scorer in Britain. Which club did he represent?**

    a) Hull

    b) Dewsbury

    c) Wigan

6. **Rugby Union. Who scored his first international try in Wales' 11-11 draw with England in 1968?**

    a) Gerald Davies

    b) Barry John

    c) Gareth Edwards

7. **Football. Which Italian club paid £70,000 for John Charles in November 1962?**

    a) Roma

    b) Inter Milan

    c) Sampdoria

8. **Cricket. Which West Indies legend played for Glamorgan between 1990 and 1993?**

9. **Athletics. Name the two Welshmen in the 4x400m Great Britain relay team that won gold in the 2002 European Championship.**

10. **Rugby Union. Which second row captained Wales for a single occasion in a 52-3 loss to New Zealand in 1988?**

# Round 27

1. **Rugby Union. Who created an unwanted record of 19 losses in his tenure in charge of Wales between 2002 and 2004?**
   a) Steve Hansen
   b) Lyn Jones
   c) Geraint John

2. **Cycling. Simon Richardson became a double gold medallist in the 2008 Paralympic Games in China. What accolade did he receive following his success?**
   a) Freedom of Porthcawl
   b) MBE
   c) Welsh sports personality of the year

3. **Football. When a certain Welshman was asked if he could see the ball during a floodlit match, his answer was 'No, I don't need to though, I can smell it'. Which cocky winger can this quote be attributed to?**
   a) Peter Sayer
   b) Tony Villars
   c) Leighton James

4. **Athletics. Who became the first ever British AAA 100m champion in 1969?**
   a) J.J. Williams
   b) Hywel Griffiths
   c) Ron Jones

5. **Rugby Union. Barney McCall's debut against England in 1936 was significant for what reason?**

    a) He became the first Welshman to score a debut try

    b) He captained Wales on his debut

    c) He became Wales' 500th international

6. **Football. Which Welshman was named Everton player of the year in the 1996/97 season?**

    a) Barry Horne

    b) Gary Speed

    c) Neville Southall

7. **Boxing. Jimmy Wilde became flyweight champion of the world in 1916. Who did he defeat via knockout to earn this title?**

    a) Young Zulu Kid

    b) Old Indian Warrior

    c) Red Apache Son

8. **Rugby Union. Name the two Llanelli Scarlets players in the 2005 British and Irish Lions squad to New Zealand.**

9. **Cricket. Wales recorded an 8 wicket victory against England in a one day international in 2002 at Sophia Gardens. Which South African international represented the home side?**

10. **Football. Who set a club record of 41 goals in a season for Swansea Town during the 1945/46 season?**

# Round 28

1. **Rugby Union. Gareth Edwards, Robert Jones and Dwayne Peel are all associated with which numbered shirt?**

   a) 9

   b) 11

   c) 13

2. **Athletics. What have Lynn Davies, Roger Hackney and Justin Chaston have in common?**

   a) They have won both Olympic and Commonwealth gold medals

   b) They have competed in three consecutive Olympic Games

   c) All three are former athletes who are now members of the Houses of Parliament

3. **Football. Ryan Green broke Ryan Giggs' record in 1998 when he became Wales' youngest ever senior international. Which club side was he registered to at the time?**

   a) Walsall

   b) West Bromwich Albion

   c) Wolverhampton Wanderers

4. **Rugby Union. Which 37 times capped international played 246 games for Swansea between 1985 and 1999?**

   a) Paul Moriaty

   b) Robert Jones

   c) Anthony Clement

5. **Golf. Who won his first European tour title with victory in the 2004 China Open in Shanghai?**

    a) Stephen Dodd

    b) Jamie Donaldson

    c) Mark Pilkington

6. **Football. Who was the only non Englishman in the Coventry City side that beat Tottenham Hotspur 3-2 in the 1987 FA Cup final?**

    a) David Phillips

    b) Mark Bowen

    c) Malcolm Allen

7. **Snooker. In 1987, which prestigious event did Darren Morgan win?**

    a) UK Championship

    b) World Amateur Championship

    c) Dubai Classic

8. **Rugby League. Jonathan Davies signed professional forms in 1988, turning his back on the union game. Which club did he join?**

9. **Boxing. Who was named BBC Wales sports personality of the year in 1956?**

10. **Football. Kevin Ratcliffe was given his first taste of football management in 1995. Which side gave him this opportunity?**

# Round 29

1. **Football. Craig Bellamy famously brandished a golf club at a Liverpool teammate during a drink fuelled argument which followed a karaoke session in 2007. Who was the other player involved in the incident?**

   a) Xabi Alonso

   b) Sami Hyypia

   c) John Arne Riise

2. **Rugby Union. Who scored 5 tries in 7 test matches for the British and Irish Lions between 1974 and 1977?**

   a) Steve Fenwick

   b) Terry Cobner

   c) J.J. Williams

3. **Cricket. In 2007, who was named as Glamorgan's cricket manager?**

   a) Matthew Maynard

   b) Steve Watkin

   c) Adrian Shaw

4. **Athletics. Who won the British AAA 100yds Championship in 1963?**

   a) Berwyn Jones

   b) Terry Davies

   c) David Griffiths

5. **Rugby Union. Who scored Wales' winning try in their 13-8 victory over the 'All Blacks' in 1953?**

   a) Cliff Morgan

   b) Ken Jones

   c) Gerwyn Williams

6. **Football. Which side did Peter Rodrigues captain to a 1-0 victory over Manchester United in the 1976 FA Cup final?**

   a) Southampton

   b) Crystal Palace

   c) Derby County

7. **Bowls. Who won silver in the women's singles at the 2006 Commonwealth Games?**

   a) Lisa Foray

   b) Shirley King

   c) Elizabeth Morgan

8. **Rugby Union. Who under the guidance of Lyn Jones won the 2006/07 Celtic League?**

9. **Rugby League. In a game against Blackpool in 1957, who set a Leeds record of 13 goals in a match?**

10. **Boxing. Which 'dark destroyer' beat Nicky Piper with an 11th round knockout, in their 1992 World Boxing Council (WBC) super middleweight title fight?**

# Round 30

1. **Athletics. Which Welsh athlete was made a Dame in the 2004 New Year's honours list?**
   a) Kay Morley
   b) Kirsty Wade
   c) Tanni Grey-Thompson

2. **Rugby Union. Which of the following teams is not based in Llanelli?**
   a) Bynea
   b) New Dock Stars
   c) St Peter's

3. **Football. Who in 1991 became the first player to win the Professional Footballers Association player of the year award twice?**
   a) Mark Hughes
   b) Ian Rush
   c) Neville Southall

4. **Ice Hockey. Which Cardiff Devils star was named 1996/97 Super League player of the year?**
   a) Mike Ware
   b) Stevie Lyle
   c) Doug McEwan

5. **Rugby League. Who was Great Britain's top points scorer on their 1970 tour of Australasia?**
    a) Tony Fisher
    b) Terry Price
    c) Clive Sullivan

6. **Rugby Union. What was significant about Wales' 6-3 defeat by Scotland in 1907?**
    a) First three point try scored by an international team
    b) Last game in which Wales fielded seven forwards and eight backs
    c) First ever Welsh defeat to Scotland

7. **Darts. Which Englishman defeated Leighton Rees in the final of the 1979 BDO World Championship final?**
    a) Keith Deller
    b) John Lowe
    c) Dave Whitcombe

8. **Cricket. Roland Lefebvre joined Glamorgan from Somerset in 1993. What was his nationality?**

9. **Football. Who scored his second Premier League goal for Reading against Middlesborough in 2007, with his first coming ten years previously for Everton against Barnsley in 1997?**

10. **Boxing. Which Carmarthen super heavyweight won silver at the 2006 Commonwealth Games?**

# Round 31

1. **Various. St Helen's, The Vetch Field and The Liberty Stadium are all grounds associated with which city?**

   a) Newport

   b) St David's

   c) Swansea

2. **Football. John Toshack formed a formidable partnership with which English player during his period at Liverpool in the 1970s?**

   a) Kevin Keegan

   b) Paul Mariner

   c) Charlie George

3. **Rugby Union. Whose 2008 autobiography was called 'The magnificent seven'.**

   a) Martyn Williams

   b) Colin Charvis

   c) Kingsley Jones

4. **Rowing. Tom James won Olympic gold at the 2008 games. Which event was he successful in?**

   a) Coxless pair

   b) Coxless four

   c) Coxless eight

5. **Cricket. In January 1930, who became Glamorgan's first ever England international test player?**
   a) Dennis Sullivan
   b) Trevor Arnott
   c) Maurice Turnbull

6. **Athletics. Which future rugby union international was Welsh javelin champion in 1953?**
   a) Garfield Owen
   b) Terry Davies
   c) Malcolm Price

7. **Horse Racing. 2008 saw Jim Dreaper provide the first Irish trained horse to win the Welsh National. What was the name of the 16-1 winner?**
   a) Cornish Sett
   b) Officier De Reserve
   c) Notre Pere

8. **Rugby League. Which club signed Allan Bateman from the union game in 1990?**

9. **Rugby Union. Name the three Welsh forwards in the 1989 British and Irish Lions squad to Australia**

10. **Football. Which Zimbabwe born utility player made his Welsh debut in a 1-1 draw against Albania in 1996?**

# Round 32

1. **Rugby Union. Which club side did J.P.R. Williams, Mervyn Davies and Keith Hughes all play for during the 1970s?**
   a) London Welsh
   b) Caerphilly
   c) Dunvant

2. **Football. Which of the following trophies did John Charles not win during his illustrious career?**
   a) Welsh Cup
   b) FA Cup
   c) Copa Italia

3. **Cycling. Nicole Cooke's gold at the 2008 Olympic Games was Great Britain's first in China. In which event did this occur?**
   a) Time trial
   b) Individual pursuit
   c) Road race

4. **Athletics. Who won the 400m World Indoor Championship in Maebashi, Japan, in 1999?**
   a) Iwan Thomas
   b) Doug Turner
   c) Jamie Baulch

5. **Boxing. What was the nickname of Cardiff's world champion boxer Steve Robinson?**
    a) Lucky Strike
    b) Cinderella Man
    c) Taff Terrier

6. **Rugby Union. Who scored five tries in the British and Irish Lions' 109-6 victory over Manawatu in 2005?**
    a) Gareth Thomas
    b) Shane Williams
    c) Tom Shanklin

7. **Rugby League. Johnny Thomas set a Welsh international record against England in 1908 which wasn't equalled for 70 years, until Paul Woods achieved the same feat against France in 1978. What was this achievement?**
    a) Kicked seven goals in a match
    b) Scored four tries in a game
    c) Captained the team to a win on his debut

8. **Cricket. Which left handed Australian opening batsman joined Glamorgan as their overseas player in 2000?**

9. **Football. Which Middle East country appointed Terry Yorath as their manager in 1995?**

10. **Rugby Union. Which centre captained Cardiff to the 1994/95 Welsh league championship?**

# Round 33

1.  **Cycling. A £7.5 million Wales National Cycling Centre was opened in 2003. Where is it located?**
    - a) Caernarfon
    - b) Newport
    - c) Burry Port

2.  **Rugby Union. Alex Evans was succeeded as Cardiff head coach in 1995 by which former scrum half?**
    - a) Brynmor Williams
    - b) Gareth Edwards
    - c) Terry Holmes

3.  **Football. Which former England international was the son of a Welsh rugby league international?**
    - a) Emlyn Hughes
    - b) David Platt
    - c) Bobby Moore

4.  **Boxing. Who became Wales' 10th world champion when he won the World Boxing Association (WBA) light welterweight crown against Souleymane M'Baye in 2007?**
    - a) Jamie Arthur
    - b) Gavin Rees
    - c) Bradley Pryce

5. **Cricket. Which side beat Glamorgan by 5 wickets in the 1977 Gillete cup final at Lords?**

    a) Middlesex

    b) Yorkshire

    c) Durham

6. **Rugby League. England were victorious 25-10 against Wales in the semi final of the 1995 World Cup. Which football ground played host to this occasion?**

    a) Elland Road

    b) Old Trafford

    c) Goodison Park

7. **Swimming. In 1912, Irene Steer became the first Welshwoman to win an Olympic gold medal. She was successful in the 4x100m freestyle. Where were these games held?**

    a) Stockholm

    b) Berlin

    c) Antwerp

8. **Rugby Union. In 1999, who became the first person to lead Wales to victory over South Africa with a 29-19 win?**

9. **Snooker. Who defeated Dennis Taylor to become 1979 World Champion?**

10. **Football. Who was the only Welshman in the Liverpool side that beat Borussia Monchengladbach 2-1, to win their first ever European Cup in 1977?**

# Round 34

1. **Football. What job did Neville Southall do before becoming a professional Footballer?**
   a) Plumber
   b) Cake decorator
   c) Binman

2. **Rugby Union. In 2009 Martyn Williams became the Welsh player with most appearances in the five/six nations. Whose 45 games total did he overtake?**
   a) Ieuan Evans
   b) Robert Jones
   c) Gareth Edwards

3. **Rugby League. Brothers Thomas, Edward and Keiron Cunningham have all played for which famous club?**
   a) St Helens
   b) Widnes
   c) Wigan

4. **Athletics. How many times did Colin Jackson win European Championship gold in the 110m hurdles?**
   a) 2
   b) 3
   c) 4

5. **Cricket. Glamorgan's first ever match was at Cardiff Arms Park in 1889. Who were the opposition?**
   a) Herefordshire
   b) Durham
   c) Warwickshire

6. **Football. Who won the Welsh Cup five times in the first ten years of the competition's history?**
   a) Druids
   b) Chirk
   c) Oswestry United

7. **Athletics. John Disley won Olympic bronze in the 1952 summer games in Helsinki. In which competition did he win this accolade?**
   a) Long Jump
   b) Marathon
   c) Steeplechase

8. **Boxing. In 2007, Joe Calzaghe became undisputed super middleweight champion of the world. Which Danish fighter did he defeat?**

9. **Football. Wales appointed their first English manager of the national side in 1974. Who was he?**

10. **Rugby Union. Who were Welsh champions for three consecutive seasons between 1988 and 1991?**

# Round 35

1. **Athletics. Lynn Davies won Olympic gold at the 1964 summer games. Which city hosted the event?**

   a) Birmingham

   b) Glasgow

   c) Tokyo

2. **Rugby Union. During the 2008/09 Heineken Cup, the Ospreys set a competition record for highest team score and winning margin with a 68-8 victory. Who were the opposition?**

   a) London Wasps

   b) Benetton Treviso

   c) Munster

3. **Football. Cliff Jones left Tottenham Hotspur in October 1968. Which club did he join for a £5,000 fee?**

   a) Fulham

   b) Arsenal

   c) Manchester United

4. **Cricket. Glamorgan won their second County Championship in 1969. Who captained this winning side?**

   a) Malcolm Nash

   b) Eifion Jones

   c) Tony Lewis

5. **Boxing. Which Swansea born boxer made three unsuccessful attempts to claim a world welterweight title between 1982 and 1985?**

   a) Colin Jones
   b) Mike Copp
   c) Frank McCord

6. **Rugby Union. Who were the two ever present Llanelli players in Wales' 1971 Grand Slam winning side?**

   a) Roy Bergiers and Derek Quinnell
   b) Barry Llewelyn and Delme Thomas
   c) Norman Gale and Phil Bennett

7. **Table Tennis. Nigeria's Segun Toriola won Commonwealth bronze at the 2006 Melbourne games. Which Welshman did he defeat in the third place decider?**

   a) Stephen Jenkins
   b) Ryan Jenkins
   c) Adam Robertson

8. **Rugby League. Who did Jonathan Griffiths play 143 matches for between 1989 and 1995?**

9. **Football. March 9th 1999 is a significant date in the history of Welsh club football, as Aston Villa signed the first former League of Wales player to an English Premiership side. Who was this former Carmarthen Town defender?**

10. **Boxing. Which Newport born boxer defeated Hans Kalbfell to claim the European heavyweight title in 1960?**

# Round 36

1.  **Football. Who scored 22 goals in 75 internationals between 1986 and 2001?**

    a) Dean Saunders

    b) Malcolm Allen

    c) Iwan Roberts

2.  **Rugby League. Who set a 26 cap Welsh record between 1921 and 1939, missing only a single game during that 18 year period?**

    a) Jim Sullivan

    b) Jerry Shea

    c) Mel Meek

3.  **Rugby Union. In 1975, who scored a hat-trick in Wales' 28-3 victory over Australia?**

    a) Clive Rees

    b) J.J. Williams

    c) Brynmor Williams

4.  **Showjumping. Name the horse ridden by gold winning medallist Harry Llewellyn at the 1952 Helsinki Olympic Games.**

    a) Foxtrotter

    b) Foxglove

    c) Foxhunter

5. **Cricket. Former Glamorgan players Haydn Davies, Eifion Jones and Colin Metson shared which discipline?**

   a) Spin bowling

   b) Wicket keeping

   c) Fast bowling

6. **Rugby Union. Who captained Wales to their 1952 Grand Slam?**

   a) John Gwilliam

   b) Lewis Jones

   c) Rees Stephens

7. **Rallying. Ebbw Vale born Nicky Grist won his first World Rally Championship race in Argentina, in 1993. Who was he co-driver to for this race?**

   a) Armin Schwarz

   b) Juha Kankkunen

   c) Dave Metcalf

8. **Rugby Union. International back rower Alix Popham left South Wales for France in the summer of 2008. Which club did he join?**

9. **Football. Two Welshmen were in the Manchester United side that won the 1991 European Cup Winners' Cup. Mark Hughes was one. Who was the other?**

10. **Golf. In 1968, who won the Harry Vardon Trophy as the leading money winner on the European tour with £8,000?**

# Round 37

1. **Golf. What was Ian Woosnam's role in Europe's 2002 Ryder Cup victory?**

   a) Captain

   b) Vice captain

   c) Caddie

2. **Football. Simon Davies made a £700,000 move from Peterborough United to the English Premier League in January 2000. Which club did he join?**

   a) Chelsea

   b) Arsenal

   c) Tottenham Hotspur

3. **Boxing. Who beat John Davison to win the vacant WBO world featherweight title following two days notice in April 1993?**

   a) Steve Robinson

   b) Nigel Haddock

   c) Peter Harris

4. **Rugby League. Who skippered Great Britain to victory in the 1972 World Cup in France?**

   a) Tony Fisher

   b) John Mantle

   c) Clive Sullivan

5. **Athletics. Which Welshwoman won silver behind England's Kelly Holmes in the 1500m at the 2002 Commonwealth Games?**

   a) Rachael Newcombe

   b) Natalie Lewis

   c) Hayley Tullett

6. **Rugby Union. Who made a try scoring debut as Wales defeated England 22-6 in 1971?**

   a) John Bevan

   b) Roy Mathias

   c) Arthur Lewis

7. **Football. Who scored his only international hat-trick in Wales' 3-2 victory over Northern Ireland in 1955?**

   a) Ivor Allchurch

   b) John Charles

   c) Terry Medwin

8. **Rugby Union. Which former Llantwit Fardre, Pontypridd, Bridgend, Cardiff and Treorchy flanker was named Cardiff Blues forwards coach in the summer of 2008?**

9. **Snooker. Which Upper Tumble born player became World Amateur Champion in 1963 and 1966?**

10. **Football. Who were the inaugural champions of the League of Wales in 1992/93?**

# Round 38

1.  **Cricket. International cricketer Herschelle Gibbs joined Glamorgan in the summer of 2008. Which country is he from?**

    a) Canada

    b) Holland

    c) South Africa

2.  **Football. Who had a 44 day spell in charge of the Welsh national side in 1994?**

    a) John Toshack

    b) Kevin Keegan

    c) Bruce Grobbelaar

3.  **Rugby League. Les White was the first, Tommy Harris the second and Tony Fisher the third Welshman to play for Great Britain at which position?**

    a) Scrum Half

    b) Wing

    c) Hooker

4.  **Rugby Union. Who captained Llanelli for six consecutive seasons between 1973 and 1979?**

    a) Phil Bennett

    b) Gareth Jenkins

    c) Ray Gravell

5. **Athletics. Christian Malcolm became a double 100m and 200m gold medallist in 1998. At which competition were these medals won?**
     a) European under 23 Championship
     b) World Junior Championship
     c) European Indoor Championship

6. **Snooker. Who won the 1989 Mercantile Credit Classic?**
     a) Darren Morgan
     b) Doug Mountjoy
     c) Terry Griffiths

7. **Horse Racing. Which Anthony brother won the Grand National three times in 1911, 1915 and 1920?**
     a) Jack
     b) Ivor
     c) Owain

8. **Football. 'Ninja' was the nickname of which Singapore born Welsh defender due to his famous brown headband?**

9. **Rugby Union. 5 times capped New Zealand hooker Tom Willis moved to Wales in the summer of 2008. Which region did he join?**

10. **Boxing. In 1995, who defeated Noel Magee to claim the Commonwealth light heavyweight title?**

# Round 39

1. **Football. Who scored 49 competitive goals and a penalty in the European Cup final shoot out to earn the 1984 European golden boot award?**

    a) Ian Rush

    b) Mark Hughes

    c) Ian Walsh

2. **Horse Racing. Hywel Davies won the Grand National at Aintree in 1985. What was the name of the horse he rode?**

    a) Ernie's Boy

    b) Dangerous Dan

    c) Last Suspect

3. **Rugby Union. During the 2008 six nations, what did Mike Phillips and Martyn Williams do against Ireland, which Gavin Henson repeated against France?**

    a) Kick a drop goal

    b) Break a leg

    c) Receive a yellow card

4. **Swimming. David Davies won bronze at the 2004 Athens Olympic Games. Which event did he achieve this?**

    a) 50m

    b) 100m

    c) 1500m

5. **Football. Peter Nicholas won a second division winner's medal in the 1988/89 season. With which club did he win this?**

    a) Chelsea

    b) Watford

    c) Luton Town

6. **Rugby Union. Which former Welsh outside half was elected president of the Welsh Rugby Union for the historic 1980/81 centenary season?**

    a) Bill Cleaver

    b) Cliff Jones

    c) Barry John

7. **Athletics. New Zealand's Roy Williams won decathlon gold at the 1966 Commonwealth Games. Who set a UK record of 7123 points in coming second?**

    a) Eirwyn Jones

    b) Goronwy Davies

    c) Clive Longe

8. **Rugby League. Neil Cowie, Kelvin Skerrett, Scott Quinnell and Martin Hall were all members of the Wales squad that reached the semi finals of the 1995 World Cup. Which club did they play for?**

9. **Football. Who was named Welsh sports personality of the year in 1962?**

10. **Rowing. Tom James competed in the University Boat Race four times, but only won it once in 2007. Which university did he represent?**

# Round 40

1.  **Football. Which goalkeeper was voted Welsh international player of the year in 1999?**

    a) Paul Jones

    b) Martyn Margetson

    c) Andy Marriott

2.  **Snooker. Before becoming a professional sportsman, which of the following occupations did Terry Griffiths not turn his hand to?**

    a) Postman

    b) Butcher

    c) Bus Conductor

3.  **Rugby Union. What record did Stephen Jones create in Wales' 43-9 defeat by England in 2003?**

    a) Fastest international penalty kick

    b) First Llanelli Scarlets regional player to captain Wales

    c) Most capped Welsh outside half

4.  **Rugby League. The European Nations Cup was held on 5 occasions in the 1930s. How many times did Wales win the competition in this period?**

    a) 1

    b) 3

    c) 5

5. **Boxing.** Who defeated Sandro Casamonica to claim the title of European lightweight champion in 2002?

   a) Tony Doherty
   b) Bradley Pryce
   c) Jason Cook

6. **Various.** In 1996, Sir Steve Redgrave won his fourth Olympic gold medal, equalling the then British record held by Welshman Paulo Radmilovic. In which sports did Radmilovic win his medals?

   a) Swimming and Water Polo
   b) Shooting and Rowing
   c) Cycling and Archery

7. **Rugby Union.** Whose try secured a memorable 12-16 victory for 14 man Cardiff Blues against Gloucester in the pool stages of the 2008/09 Heineken Cup?

   a) Jamie Roberts
   b) Andy Powell
   c) Bradley Davies

8. **Weightlifting.** Who won 2 gold medals at the 2002 Commonwealth Games, taking his tally to 9 gold medals, having won his first at the age of 17 in 1982?

9. **Football.** Who did Dave Sexton mistakenly name in the England under 21 squad during the 1993/94 season even though he had already played for Wales under 21 level?

10. **Athletics.** Kay Morley won Commonwealth gold at the Auckland games of 1990. In which event was this medal won?

# Round 41

1. **Rugby Union. Which Swansea player captained Wales to a first ever run of five defeats between 1989 and 1990?**

   a) Anthony Clement

   b) Robert Jones

   c) Arthur Emyr

2. **Cricket. Which Glamorgan player was a member of the England team that won the 2005 Ashes series against Australia?**

   a) Simon Jones

   b) Mike Powell

   c) Alex Wharf

3. **Football. Leighton James spent three spells with the same club during his career. Which club?**

   a) Real Madrid

   b) Burnley

   c) Derby County

4. **Rugby League. Who replaced Martin Hall as Wales coach in 2008?**

   a) Justin Morgan

   b) Kevin Ellis

   c) John Dixon

5. **Athletics. For four successive years from 1949 to 1952, the Welsh triple jump championship went to a future Rugby union international. Who was he?**
   a) Trevor Brewer
   b) Alun Thomas
   c) Gordon Wells

6. **Boxing. What have Jack Peterson, Joe Erskine, David Pearce and Scott Gammer have in common?**
   a) They were all British heavyweight champion
   b) They were all European heavyweight champion
   c) All four are Olympic gold medallists

7. **Darts. Raymond Van Barneveld became BDO world champion for the third time in 2003. Who did he defeat in the final 6-3?**
   a) Ritchie Davies
   b) Marshall James
   c) Richie Burnett

8. **Rugby Union. Why was Cardiff's 33-26 victory over Swansea in the 1997 Welsh cup final historically more significant than other cup finals?**

9. **Athletics. Wales won bronze in the 4x400m at the 1998 Commonwealth Games in Kuala Lumpur. Name the quartet.**

10. **Football. Wrexham signed Lee Trundle in 2000 from which Welsh club side?**

# Round 42

1. **Rugby Union. Where was Wales' 2008, 16-12 victory over Ireland played?**
   a) Ravenhill
   b) Croke Park
   c) Twickenham

2. **Football. Who was sent off for the first time in his career during Wales' 3-2 defeat by Norway in September 2001?**
   a) Robbie Savage
   b) Robert Page
   c) Ryan Giggs

3. **Boxing. Jim Driscoll became European champion in 1912. At which weight was this title won?**
   a) Heavyweight
   b) Welterweight
   c) Featherweight

4. **Swimming. Tanni Grey-Thompson's British Paralympic record of 11 gold medals was equalled in 2008. Which Welsh swimmer matched her feat?**
   a) David Roberts
   b) Rhiannon Henry
   c) Gareth Duke

5. **Rugby Union. In 1994, Ieuan Evans broke the record for most appearances as Welsh captain with his 19th game in the role. The previous record had stood since 1897. Who held the record?**

   a) William Bancroft

   b) Arthur Gould

   c) Henry Simpson

6. **Snooker. Who defeated Jimmy White in the final of the first ever professional players' grand prix tournament in 1982?**

   a) Ray Reardon

   b) Terry Griffiths

   c) Doug Mountjoy

7. **Athletics. Which competition saw David Jacobs win Olympic gold in 1912, Ken Jones win silver in 1948 and Nick Whitehead take bronze in 1960?**

   a) Long Jump

   b) Decathlon

   c) Sprint relay

8. **Football. 'Hard man, hard knocks' was an autobiography published in 2004 about which former Welsh captain and manager?**

9. **Rugby League. Which Welsh winger was released by St Helens at the end of the 2001 season having scored 213 tries in 305 appearances?**

10. **Cricket. In 1998, which former Glamorgan captain was appointed President of the Marylebone Cricket Club (MCC)?**

# Round 43

1. **Golf. What did Dai Rees do five times between 1955 and 1967, that Brian Huggett did in 1977 and Ian Woosnam did in 2006?**
    a) Win the Open championship
    b) Captain a Ryder Cup side
    c) Was disqualified in the US Open

2. **Cricket. Who captained Glamorgan to the 1997 County Championship title?**
    a) Matthew Maynard
    b) Hugh Morris
    c) Tony Cottey

3. **Rugby Union. Which legendary scrum half made his debut at the age of 18 in Wales' 13-12 victory over New Zealand in 1935?**
    a) Wick Powell
    b) Bryn Evans
    c) Haydn Tanner

4. **Football. Who captained Cardiff City to a 1-0 victory in the 1927 FA Cup final against Arsenal?**
    a) James Nelson
    b) Fred Keenor
    c) Tom Sloane

5. **Rugby League. Having finished his career with Wigan, Billy Boston came out of retirement in 1970 and played a further 11 games. Who did he make these appearances with?**

   a) Blackpool Borough
   b) Hunslet
   c) Bradford Northern

6. **Rugby Union. In which year did Wales win their first triple crown?**

   a) 1893
   b) 1913
   c) 1933

7. **Athletics. Who set a Welsh record of 20.29 seconds to win 200m silver at the 1998 Commonwealth Games?**

   a) Jamie Baulch
   b) Doug Turner
   c) Christian Malcolm

8. **Football. Which controversial midfielder made a £1.5m move from Blackburn Rovers to Derby County in January 2008?**

9. **Rugby Union. Who was the Llanelli try scoring Outside Half, in their 19-16 victory over Australia on the 20th of November 1984?**

10. **Rugby League. Who captained Wales to the semi final of the 2000 World Cup before losing to Australia 46-22?**

# Round 44

1. **Boxing. Which future world champion made his professional debut on the undercard of the Frank Bruno v Lennox Lewis world heavyweight championship fight in 1993?**

   a) Steve Robinson

   b) Joe Calzaghe

   c) Barry Jones

2. **Rugby Union. Which Welshman was an assistant coach on the 2005 British and Irish Lions tour of New Zealand?**

   a) Gareth Jenkins

   b) Kevin Hopkins

   c) Jonathan Humphreys

3. **Football. What did Mark Hughes achieve with Manchester United in 1992, with Chelsea in 1998 and with Blackburn Rovers in 2002?**

   a) Premier League top goal scorer

   b) Won the FA Cup

   c) Won the League Cup

4. **Weightlifting. How many gold medals did Andrew Davies win at the 1990 Commonwealth Games?**

   a) 1

   b) 2

   c) 3

5. **Rugby Union. Who missed a 'last kick of the match' penalty that would have given Wales a draw, in their 19-16 defeat by New Zealand in 1972?**

  a) Phil Bennett
  b) J.P.R. Williams
  c) Gareth Edwards

6. **Rugby League. Which Welsh 100 yards champion signed professional terms with Wakefield Trinity in April 1964?**

  a) Dewi Roberts
  b) Ron Jones
  c) Berwyn Jones

7. **Shooting. Which event provided Johanne Brekke with Commonwealth Games bronze in 2006?**

  a) 50m Rifle Prone
  b) 10m Air Rifle
  c) Double Trap

8. **Rugby Union. Who was named International Rugby Board world player of the year in 2008?**

9. **Snooker. Who was world champion 6 times between 1970 and 1978?**

10. **Football. Which North Wales side won the 1993/94 and 1994/95 League of Wales title?**

# Round 45

1. **Golf. Which Welsh venue was named in 2001 as host of the 2010 Ryder Cup?**
    a) Celtic Manor Resort, Newport
    b) Raglan Parc, Raglan
    c) Tyddyn Mawr, Llanrug

2. **Rugby League. The Welsh side that took to the field against England at Salford in 1968 contained 13 new caps. What was the reason for this?**
    a) The professional clubs would not release any players, hence the team was made of lower league semi professionals
    b) From 1953 to 1968 no full internationals were played by Wales
    c) Coach Griff Jenkins was so angry by their previous year's loss to England that he dropped the entire squad

3. **Rallying. Nicky Grist finished second in the 1997 World Rally Championship with 5 victories. Who was he co-driver to?**
    a) Mikael Ericsson
    b) Malcolm Wilson
    c) Colin McRae

4. **Football. Which English side reached the final of the 1992 Welsh Cup before losing 1-0 to Cardiff City?**
    a) Hednesford Town
    b) Bristol Rovers
    c) Kidderminster Harriers

5. **Rugby Union. What name was Old Monktonians Rugby club changed to in 1913?**

   a) Newport

   b) Glamorgan Wanderers

   c) Monmouth

6. **Athletics. Which Welsh title did Brychan Jones win on 4 occasions from 1981 to 1984?**

   a) Pole Vault

   b) High Jump

   c) 200m

7. **Darts. Who became the women's WDA World Cup singles champion in 2007?**

   a) Jan Robbins

   b) Sandra Greatbatch

   c) Julie Gore

8. **Football. Who were the two future Welsh internationals in the Wimbledon side that beat Liverpool 1-0 in the 1988 FA Cup final?**

9. **Boxing. Who defeated Tony Oakey in 2008 to claim the vacant Commonwealth Light Heavyweight title?**

10. **Cricket. Who recorded Glamorgan's best ever bowling figures of 7-16 in a one day contest, against Surrey in 1998?**

# Round 46

1. **Football. Which teenager made a £10 million transfer from Southampton to Tottenham Hotspur in May 2007?**
   a) Chris Gunter
   b) Gareth Bale
   c) Jack Collison

2. **Rugby Union. For what reason will Rob Higgitt go down in Stradey Park history?**
   a) He made the most club appearances at the ground
   b) He was the only person to have played for 5 different teams at Stradey Park
   c) He was the last ever try scorer at Stradey Park

3. **Athletics. What milestone did Bob Maplestone achieve in San Diego in February 1972?**
   a) First British athlete to run a mile indoors under 4 minutes
   b) First European to win an American college title
   c) First Welshman to compete for America through dual nationality

4. **Cricket. Which feat did John Bell achieve while playing against Worcestershire in 1926?**
   a) First person to make 300 Glamorgan appearances
   b) First Glamorgan player to score a double century

c) First Glamorgan player to score 1,000 runs
   in a season

5. **Rugby Union. Whose last minute penalty gave the Welsh women a 16-15 first ever victory over England in 2009?**

   a) Non Evans
   b) Naomi Thomas
   c) Amy Day

6. **Rugby League. Wales' European Nations Cup victory in 1995 was their first since which year?**

   a) 1938
   b) 1958
   c) 1978

7. **Judo. The 1990 Commonwealth Games saw Judo appear for the first time as an event. Who in the extra light category was Wales' only silver medallist?**

   a) Helen Duston
   b) James Charles
   c) Lisa Griffiths

8. **Rugby Union. In the 1975/76 season, which number eight was named Welsh player of the year for the second successive season?**

9. **Football. Matthew Jones was signed by Peter Taylor for £3.25 million from Leeds in 2000. Which club did he join?**

10. **Tennis. Who partnered Bob Wilson to the final of the 1960 Wimbledon men's doubles final before narrowly losing to Rafael Osuna and Dennis Ralston?**

# Round 47

1. **Rugby Union. Which position would you associate with Dewi Bebb, Nigel Walker and Chris Czekaj?**

   a) Wing

   b) Scrum Half

   c) Flanker

2. **Boxing. Who defeated Juan Rodriguez in 1980 to claim the European Bantamweight title?**

   a) Colin Miles

   b) Johnny Owen

   c) Glyn Davies

3. **Football. Who in 2006 became the first player to make 500 Premier League appearances?**

   a) Mark Pembridge

   b) Gary Speed

   c) Robbie Savage

4. **Snooker. In 1999, who captained Wales to victory in the Nations Cup?**

   a) Dominic Dale

   b) Mark Williams

   c) Darren Morgan

5. **Rugby League. Who was the only Leeds player in Wales' 1995 World Cup squad?**

    a) Richard Eyres

    b) Adrian Hadley

    c) Scott Gibbs

6. **Cricket. In 1890, Herbie Morgan created which record against Monmouthshire?**

    a) First England test player to represent Glamorgan

    b) First Glamorgan player to score a century

    c) First Glamorgan bowler to take 10 wickets an innings

7. **Bowls. Robert Weale won silver at the 2006 Commonwealth Games. In which event was this medal won?**

    a) Singles

    b) Pairs

    c) Triples

8. **Athletics. In 1990, whose 27 year Welsh 100 metres record did Colin Jackson break?**

9. **Football. Name the Welshman who played in the Manchester United side that defeated Brighton and Hove Albion 4-0 in the 1983 FA Cup final replay?**

10. **Rugby Union. What did Bleddyn Williams do with Cardiff on the 12th of November 1953, which he did again 4 weeks later with Wales?**

# Round 48

1. **Rugby League. Which of the following clubs did Jonathan Davies not play for in his time in Rugby league?**

   a) Warrington

   b) Wigan

   c) Widnes

2. **Rugby Union. Ieuan Evans, Neil Boobyer, Nigel Davies and Wayne Proctor formed the Welsh three quarter line against Fiji in a 23-8 win in 1994. Which club did they all play for?**

   a) Llanelli

   b) Pontypridd

   c) Neath

3. **Boxing. Joe Calzaghe added the International Boxing Federation (IBF) super middleweight belt to his WBO crown in 2006. Which American did he defeat to gain this title?**

   a) Jeff Lacy

   b) Jermain Taylor

   c) Oscar De La Hoya

4. **Athletics. Which event saw Julie Crane claim silver at the 2006 Commonwealth Games?**

   a) 200 metres

   b) Javelin

   c) High Jump

5. **Football. Who scored Cardiff City's goal in their 1-0 FA Cup victory over Arsenal in 1927?**

   a) Sam Irving
   b) Hughie Ferguson
   c) Len Davies

6. **Various. What did Viv Huzzey do in 1908, which Jack Wetter did in 1920, which David Bishop and Mark Ring both did in 1984?**

   a) Become dual sport Welsh internationals in Baseball and Rugby Union
   b) Play Davis Cup Tennis for Great Britain
   c) Win junior football caps for the Republic of Ireland, before winning a senior rugby union cap for Wales

7. **Athletics. Who won silver at the 1948 London Olympic Games in the marathon?**

   a) Ken Jones
   b) Tom Richards
   c) Ron Jones

8. **Rugby Union. Which Cardiff Blues winger became the 60th teenager to be capped by Wales when he made his international debut against South Africa in 2008?**

9. **Football. Which club did goalkeeper Gary Sprake make 507 first team appearances for, from 1962 to 1973?**

10. **Darts. Wales became the first country to win the WDF team World Cup in 1972. Name the 3 team members.**

# Round 49

1. **Football. Who became Swansea City manager following the departure of Kenny Jackett in February 2007?**
   - a) Ruud Gullit
   - b) Roberto Martinez
   - c) Jurgen Klinsman

2. **Rugby Union. Who scored Wales' only try in their 21-16 defeat to France in February 2009?**
   - a) Lee Byrne
   - b) Shane Williams
   - c) Stephen Jones

3. **Athletics. Which Welsh title did Jamie Baulch win on 4 consecutive occasions from 1991 to 1994?**
   - a) Long Jump championship
   - b) 100m championship
   - c) 200m championship

4. **Football. What was unusual about the international careers of brothers David and John Hollins?**
   - a) They both won 27 caps and played together in each game
   - b) David played for Wales while John played for England
   - c) They became the first set of brothers to play together in a Welsh side

5. **Boxing. British and Empire heavyweight champion Jack Peterson lost only 5 professional fights in his career. 4 of these losses were to the same person. Who was he?**

a) Len Harvey

b) Walter Neusel

c) Jack Doyle

**6. Cricket. Glamorgan's Mark Wallace made his debut against Somerset at the end of the 1999 season. What record did he create?**

a) At 17 years and 287 days he became Glamorgan's youngest County Championship wicket keeper

b) He became the first Glamorgan player to score a double century on his debut

c) He became the first Glamorgan player to captain a County Championship side on his first team debut

**7. Snooker. Who lost in the final of the 1969 World Championship to John Spencer?**

a) Cliff Wilson

b) Ray Reardon

c) Gary Owen

**8. Football. Which colourful midfielder was given an 18 month sentence in 1993 for passing counterfeit money to trainees at Wrexham Football club?**

**9. Rugby Union. Who controversially had his try disallowed for 'rabbiting over the line' with 15 minutes to go in Wales' 19-16 defeat to New Zealand in 1972?**

**10. Diving. Who won Commonwealth Games gold at the 1990 games in the men's high dive?**

# Round 50

1. **Rugby Union. The Bridge Field is home to which club side?**

   a) Ebbw Vale
   b) Llanelli
   c) Bedwas

2. **Football. Which English midfielder had a loan spell at Swansea City during the 1995/96 season, making 9 appearances and scoring a goal?**

   a) Steven Gerrard
   b) Frank Lampard
   c) Paul Scholes

3. **Cricket. Matthew Maynard made his Glamorgan debut against Yorkshire in 1985. What happened on this occasion?**

   a) He ran out 3 colleagues in the same innings
   b) He scored a debut century
   c) He broke his wrist resulting in him missing
      the rest of the season

4. **Rugby Union. Who scored a try and drop goal in Cardiff's 14-8 victory over Australia in 1966?**

   a) Billy Hullin
   b) Gerald Davies
   c) Maurice Richards

5. **Darts. At Rosmalen, The Netherlands, in 2007, who became WDF male singles World Cup champion?**
    a) Richie Burnett
    b) Martin Phillips
    c) Mark Webster

6. **Golf. Who did Phillip Price beat in the singles of the 2002 Ryder Cup at The Belfry?**
    a) Paul Azinger
    b) David Duval
    c) Phil Mickelson

7. **Cycling. Why did Don Skene, winning bronze in the 10 mile track race at the 1954 Empire and Commonwealth Games place him in the record books?**
    a) At 18, he became the games' youngest cycling medallist
    b) He became the first person to win a gold, silver and bronze at the same championship
    c) He set a European record which stood for 23 years

8. **Athletics. Who won Commonwealth gold in the long jump at the 1966 and 1970 games?**

9. **Football. In 1986 which defender became Wales' most capped international passing the previous record of 68 held by Ivor Allchurch?**

10. **Rugby Union. Which Llanelli Outside Half became Wales' 900th international when he took to the field against Ireland in 1992?**

# *Answers*

## Round 1

1. a
2. a
3. c
4. b
5. a
6. b
7. c
8. Martyn Woodruffe
9. Arsenal
10. Kevin Morgan, Neil Jenkins and Gareth Wyatt

## Round 2

1. a
2. c
3. c
4. b
5. c
6. b
7. a
8. Gus Risman
9. Vinnie Jones
10. David Young

## Round 3

1. a
2. a
3. b
4. b
5. c
6. b
7. b
8. Kirsty Wade
9. Eifion Williams
10. Gareth Thomas and Mefin Davies

## Round 4

1. c
2. c
3. a
4. b
5. a
6. c
7. a
8. Mark Williams and Matthew Stevens. Williams won 10-8
9. Rhys Weston
10. Shaun Pickering

## Round 5

1. a
2. c
3. b
4. c
5. c
6. a

7. c

8. Jonathan Jones

9. Carl Llewellyn

10. Huw Richards

## Round 6

1. b

2. c

3. b

4. a

5. b

6. c

7. c

8. Pat Van Den Hauwe

9. Arthur Lewis

10. Sally Hodge

## Round 7

1. a

2. a

3. c

4. c

5. a

6. c

7. b

8. Doug Turner

9. Jim Sullivan

10. Martyn Jordan won three Welsh caps while Charles Jordan won a single Irish cap

## Round 8

1. c
2. b
3. b
4. b
5. c
6. a
7. b
8. J.P.R. Williams
9. Ossie Wheatley
10. Barry Jones

## Round 9

1. c
2. c
3. b
4. b
5. a
6. a
7. b
8. Howard Winstone
9. Junior Wimbledon
10. Billy Bancroft (33 caps) and Jack Bancroft (18 caps).

## Round 10

1. b
2. c
3. b
4. b
5. a
6. a

7. b

8. Stephen Jones, a conversion

9. Jeff Hammond

10. Maldwyn Lewis Evans

## Round 11

1. b

2. b

3. a

4. b

5. a

6. b

7. c

8. Cliff Wilson

9. Rhondda Rebels

10. Michael Kasprowicz

## Round 12

1. c

2. a

3. b

4. c

5. b

6. b

7. b

8. Bleddyn Williams

9. David Broome

10. Graham Gibbs was 1965 Welsh pole vault champion, his son Scott scored the winning try for Wales against England in 1999.

## Round 13

1. c
2. a
3. a
4. b
5. c
6. b
7. c
8. Dafydd James and Scott Quinnell
9. Waqar Younis
10. Valerie Davies

## Round 14

1. b
2. c
3. c
4. b
5. c
6. c
7. a
8. Christian Malcolm
9. Duncan Fletcher
10. Freddie Williams

## Round 15

1. a
2. a
3. b
4. c
5. b
6. b
7. a

8. Lynn Davies
9. Chelsea player of the year
10. Terry Cobner

## Round 16

1. a
2. b
3. c
4. b
5. a
6. c
7. b
8. Kelly Morgan
9. Mike Walker
10. Johnny Williams

## Round 17

1. c
2. b
3. c
4. c
5. b
6. c
7. a
8. South Africa
9. Louise Jones
10. Aston Villa

## Round 18

1. b
2. a
3. c, a penalty kick

4. c

5. a

6. c

7. a

8. Mark Webster

9. Kenny Dalglish

10. Adrian Dale

## Round 19

1. a

2. b

3. b

4. a

5. a

6. b

7. b

8. Mark Hughes

9. Matt Elias

10. Paul John

## Round 20

1. c

2. b

3. c

4. a

5. a

6. b

7. c

8. Steve Barry

9. Wimbledon

10. Ieuan Evans

## Round 21

1. a
2. a
3. c
4. b
5. c
6. c
7. b
8. John Charles
9. Berwyn Price
10. Cardiff

## Round 22

1. b
2. b
3. a
4. c
5. a
6. c
7. b
8. Mike England
9. Brian Williams, Kevin Phillips and Jeremy Pugh
10. Prince Naseem Hamed

## Round 23

1. c
2. b
3. a
4. a
5. a
6. c
7. b

8. Brynmor Williams

9. Terry Medwin

10. Matthew Maynard

## Round 24

1. b

2. c

3. b

4. a

5. c

6. c

7. b

8. David Beckham

9. Steve James

10. Lee Byrne and Mike Phillips

## Round 25

1. a

2. b

3. c, Colin Jackson won gold while Paul Gray won bronze

4. c

5. a

6. b

7. c

8. Gwyndaf Evans

9. Stuart Davies, Rob Appleyard and Colin Charvis

10. Light flyweight

## Round 26

1. b

2. b

3. b

4. a

5. c

6. c

7. a

8. Viv Richards

9. Matt Elias and Jamie Baulch

10. Robert Norster

## Round 27

1. a

2. b

3. c

4. c

5. c

6. b

7. a

8. Dwayne Peel and Simon Easterby

9. Jacques Kallis

10. Trevor Ford

## Round 28

1. a

2. b

3. c

4. c

5. a

6. a

7. b

8. Widnes

9. Joe Erskine

10. Chester City

## Round 29

1. c
2. c
3. a
4. a
5. b
6. a
7. c
8. Ospreys
9. Lewis Jones
10. Nigel Benn

## Round 30

1. c
2. c
3. a
4. b
5. b, with 117 points
6. b
7. b
8. Dutch
9. John Oster
10. Kevin Evans

## Round 31

1. c
2. a
3. a
4. b
5. c
6. a
7. c

8. Warrington
9. David Young, Mike Griffiths and Robert Norster
10. John Robinson

## Round 32

1. a
2. b
3. c
4. c
5. b
6. b
7. a
8. Matthew Elliott
9. Lebanon
10. Mike Hall

## Round 33

1. b
2. c
3. a, his father was Fred Hughes
4. b
5. a
6. b
7. a
8. Robert Howley
9. Terry Griffiths
10. Joey Jones

## Round 34

1. c
2. c
3. a

4. c

5. c

6. a

7. c

8. Mikkel Kessler

9. Mike Smith

10. Neath

## Round 35

1. c

2. b

3. a

4. c

5. a

6. b

7. c

8. St Helens

9. Mark Delaney

10. Dick Richardson

## Round 36

1. a

2. a

3. b

4. c

5. b

6. a

7. b

8. Brive

9. Clayton Blackmore

10. Brian Huggett

## Round 37

1. b
2. c
3. a
4. c
5. c
6. a
7. b
8. Justin Burnell
9. Gary Owen
10. Cwmbran Town

## Round 38

1. c
2. a
3. c
4. a
5. b
6. b
7. a
8. Eric Young
9. Newport Gwent Dragons
10. Nicky Piper

## Round 39

1. a
2. c
3. c
4. c
5. a
6. b
7. c

8. Wigan

9. Ivor Allchurch

10. Cambridge

## Round 40

1. a

2. b

3. b

4. b

5. c

6. a, swimming in 1908, water polo in 1908, 1912 and 1920

7. c

8. David Morgan

9. John Hartson

10. 100m hurdles

## Round 41

1. b

2. a

3. b

4. c

5. c

6. a

7. a

8. This was the last match at the National Stadium, Cardiff Arms Park

9. Jamie Baulch, Paul Gray, Doug Turner and Iwan Thomas

10. Rhyl

## Round 42

1. b
2. c
3. c
4. a
5. b
6. a
7. c
8. Terry Yorath
9. Anthony Sullivan
10. Tony Lewis

## Round 43

1. b
2. a
3. c
4. b
5. a
6. a
7. c
8. Robbie Savage
9. Gary Pearce
10. Iestyn Harris

## Round 44

1. b
2. a
3. c
4. c
5. a
6. c
7. a

8. Shane Williams

9. Ray Reardon

10. Bangor City

## Round 45

1. a

2. b

3. c

4. a

5. b

6. a

7. a

8. Eric Young and Vinnie Jones

9. Nathan Cleverly

10. Darren Thomas

## Round 46

1. b

2. c, Llanelli Scarlets beat Bristol 27-0 in October 2008

3. a

4. b

5. a

6. a

7. a

8. Mervyn Davies

9. Leicester City

10. Michael Davies

## Round 47

1. a

2. b

3. b

4. c

5. a

6. b

7. a

8. Ron Jones

9. Alan Davies

10. Captained the respected side to victory over New Zealand

## Round 48

1. b

2. a

3. a

4. c

5. b

6. a, David Bishop being the only one who won a baseball cap first

7. b

8. Leigh Halfpenny

9. Leeds United

10. Leighton Rees, Alan Evans and David Jones

## Round 49

1. b

2. a

3. c

4. b

5. b

6. a

7. c

8. Mickey Thomas

9. J.P.R. Williams

10. Robert Morgan

1. c
2. b
3. b
4. a
5. c
6. c
7. a
8. Lynn Davies
9. Joey Jones, he made a total of 72 Welsh appearances
10. Colin Stephens

# Also available from Y Lolfa

Everyone in Wales thinks they know it all when it comes to the oval ball! This is a chance to see if you really do.

**£3.95**
ISBN 9781847710499

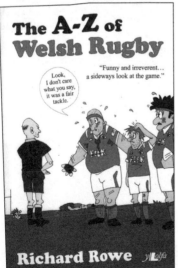

Tales of drunkenness and silliness abound in this remarkable field study. The author courageously dives head-first into the rough-and-tumble of Welsh rugby to investigate diverse aspects of the sport.

**£3.95**
ISBN 9780862439484

This book is just one of a whole range
of publications from Y Lolfa. For a full
list of books currently in print, send now
for your free copy of our new full-colour
catalogue. Or simply surf into our website

## www.ylolfa.com

for secure on-line ordering.

TALYBONT CEREDIGION CYMRU SY24 5AP
*e-mail* ylolfa@ylolfa.com
*website* www.ylolfa.com
*phone* (01970) 832 304
*fax* 832 782